SP

FILM AND VIDEO

Contents

ISBN: 531–19020–X
Library of Congress Catalog Card No. 85–52383

Published in 1986 by Warwick Press, 387 Park Avenue South, New York, NY 10016
First published in 1986 by Kingfisher Books Limited
Copyright © by Piper Books Limited 1986
Printed by Printer Portuguesa in Portugal
All rights reserved
5 4 3 2 1

FILM AND VIDEO

by
Terry Staples

Editor: Deri Warren
Designer: David Jefferis

A Gateway Fact Book
Warwick Press
New York/London/Toronto/Sydney
1986

Moving Pictures

In 1995, the movies will be 100 years old. December 28, 1895 was the first date on which an audience actually paid to watch smoothly-moving photographic images **projected** onto a screen. The show, which took place in Paris, cost one franc per person and lasted 20 minutes.

The new invention was an instant success. By 1910 the motion picture industry was already large, and growing. It had created its first "stars." During the 1920s and '30s, millions of people all over the world went to the movies every week. Most of the motion pictures were made simply to entertain. Others contained information, propaganda or social protest.

After World War II, however, things changed. The movie industry had to compete with television, which was now being transmitted in many countries. To try and win audiences, moviemakers introduced better sound and bigger

Above: During the 1930s and '40s, weekly movie-going was a habit for millions of people all over the world.

screens. They also invented gimmicks such as 3-D.

Today, blockbusters such as the **Star Wars** movies can still pack the movie theaters. But overall, moviegoing is declining. In the 1980s, people in North America go to the movies about six times a year; in Europe they go between two and three times. It seems that if the movies are going to survive their 100th birthday, they may be in a different form from that which we are used to.

The Rise of Video

Video may seem to be a recent invention, but it is older than you think. Videodiscs were on sale as early as 1938.

Video was originally developed for use in television. But in recent years it has become possible to project videos. Audiences can now watch a video production on a large screen. This means that movies are being challenged on their home ground.

Seeing is Deceiving

When we go to the movies, or watch a TV program at home, we expect to see movement on the screen. What actually happens is a little different. The movement takes place inside our minds. This is because of something we call "persistence of vision." It works something like this: Our eyes normally keep an impression of anything we look at for about one-thirtieth of a second after we move our eyes away from it. So, if we are shown a series of still pictures in very quick succession, each blends into the next. The result, to our eyes, is a moving picture.

Flip Book Pictures
You can try this out yourself by making a "flip book". Take a small blank pad or notebook. On the same spot on each page draw a simple stick figure. But make each one slightly different by changing the position of an arm or a leg, or both. Make as many drawings as possible. When you have finished, flip over the pages smoothly and rapidly. The stick figure will appear to be waving, or

kicking, or whatever you have drawn.

Both movies and video depend on persistence of vision. Without it they could not create the illusion of movement. Just as you drew a sequence of still pictures, a movie camera records action by taking 24 different still photographs per second. These photographs (known as **frames**) are later passed through a projector. They go through at the same speed.

A video image on TV is made up in the same way. Video works at a different rate from film. This rate is not standard throughout the world. In North America, for example, the image is formed, broken up, and re-formed 60 times a second. But in Europe the rate is 50 times a second.

It may sound as though video shows more than twice as many frames as film. But this is not so, because each frame is shown twice. The actual number of different frames screened per second is 30 in North America and 25 in Europe.

9

Spots and Ghosts

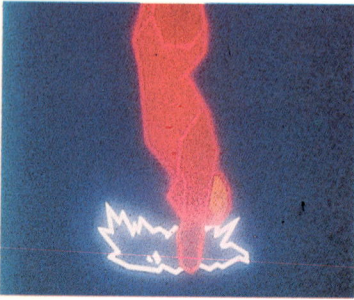

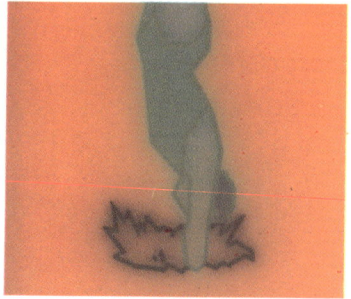

Above: Films occasionally use negatives to create unusual effects, but normally a positive print is needed.

Film is produced chemically. Video is produced electronically. This is the main difference between them. Film usually results in a clearer, better-quality image. Video, on the other hand, is faster and cheaper.

How Film Works

During filming, the film is passed through the camera. There it is exposed to light. It must then be sent to a laboratory for processing. This is what makes film slower to produce than video, which does not need to be processed.

First the film must be developed. To do this, it is soaked in chemicals. This produces a negative. A negative shows an image of the subject, not in its original colors, but in its opposite colors. Thus, blue becomes yellow, green becomes magenta, and red becomes cyan (greenish-blue).

This negative could be projected, but it would create a ghostly effect. Normally a positive print is made for projection. The colors seen on the screen are now the same as those of the original.

Layers of Light

All the colors we see on film are made by mixing just three colors – red, blue, and green light. For example, when red and green overlap, they produce yellow.

Modern color film is made up of several parts. In the middle of a strip of film is the **base**. This is there simply to provide a surface for the other components. It is usually made of plastic. Attached to one side of the base are four **emulsions**. An emulsion is a thin layer of a light-sensitive chemcial. One of these emulsions is specially made to be sensitive to blue light. Another is green-sensitive, while a third is red-sensitive.

The fourth layer of emulsion is yellow. It has a different job to do. Instead of recording light, it blocks it. It stops any blue light that may have gotten past the blue-sensitive layer from leaking in with the red and green light. Finally, there is a **backing strip** on the other side of the base. It is there to prevent any light that has passed through all the emulsions from bouncing back and destroying the clarity of the image.

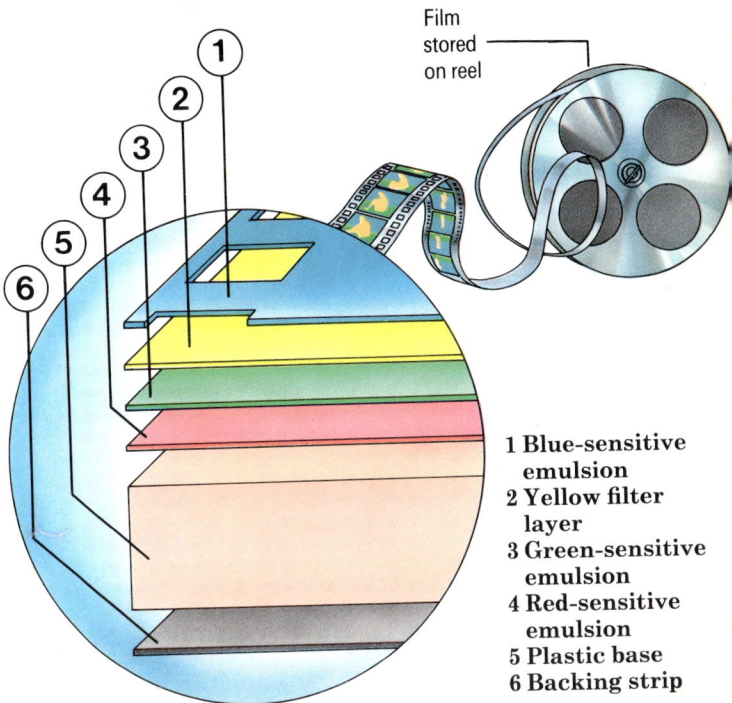

Film stored on reel

1 Blue-sensitive emulsion
2 Yellow filter layer
3 Green-sensitive emulsion
4 Red-sensitive emulsion
5 Plastic base
6 Backing strip

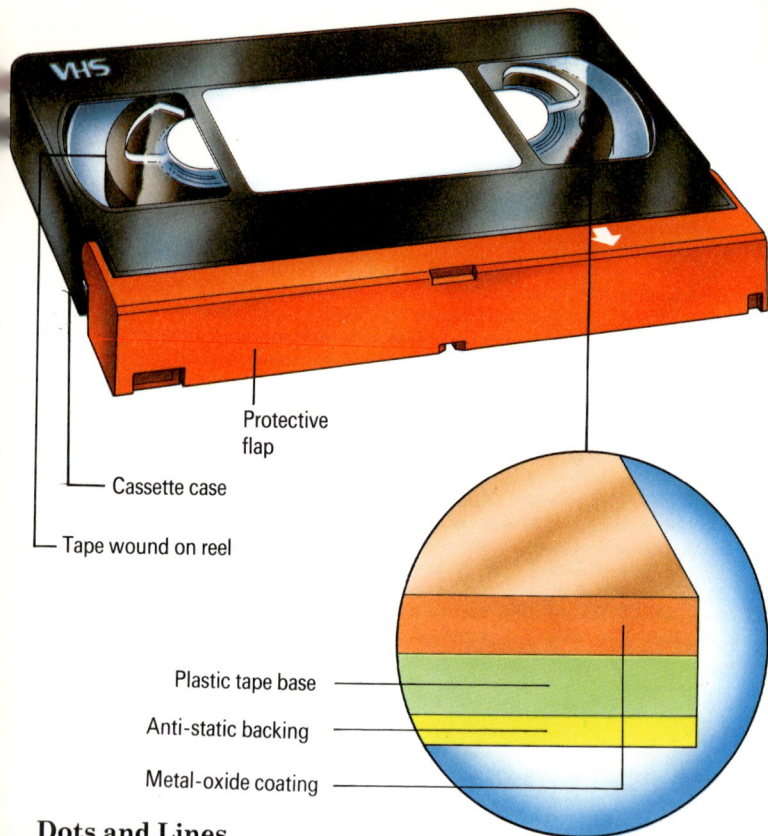

Protective
flap

Cassette case

Tape wound on reel

Plastic tape base

Anti-static backing

Metal-oxide coating

Dots and Lines

A picture that we see on television is created in an entirely different way. Look closely at a TV screen when it is turned off. Stare at a corner of it for a few seconds, and you will see that it is made of thousands of dots. Then turn on the TV. You will see lots of parallel lines endlessly racing across the screen.

**Above: A video cassette,
Inset: Cross section of a
piece of videotape.**

The dots and lines work in the same way, whether the picture is coming from a "live" broadcast, or from video playback. They are the result of a system that is known as **scanning**.

Scanning is an electronic process. A controlled beam of **electrons** sweeps across the inside of the screen. As it does so, the electrons hit the light-sensitive dots that coat the screen. They cause the dots to glow in particular colors, some brighter, some less bright. This scanning is done so fast that it is not noticeable when we watch a TV program.

Instant Playback

Video is simply a method of recording the electronic signals so that they can be played back again later. The signals are recorded on magnetic tape. As soon as the tape has been rewound, it is ready for playback. The sound, too, is automatically recorded alongside the pictures. In this way the soundtrack is always **synchronized** with the image.

The pictures recorded on videotape are not always as clear as they would be on film. But the immediacy of video is often a big advantage. For this reason, many "rock videos" are first shot on film, for quality. Then they are recorded onto video, for ease of playback.

The tape on which video signals are recorded has, like film, a plastic base. But videotape has only two extra layers. On one side of the base is a layer of metal-oxide particles. These are used to record the video sound and picture (see page 45). On the other side is a layer of carbon. It prevents a buildup of static electricity which would ruin the picture.

Below: A TV picture is composed of thousands of little phosphor dots that coat the inside of the screen.

Film and the Movies

The 1895 film show that marked the birth of the "movies" did two things. First, it took the new invention of photography a step further. Second, it made use of projection. People had been using projection for at least two hundred years. It began when somebody realized that if an object is placed in front of a source of bright light, its image will be thrown forward onto a wall or a screen.

By the second half of the 1800s, the use of projection was highly developed. Originally, flickering candlelight had been used to project the image. This was replaced by **limelight**. Limelight was so intense it could project an image from one end of a large public hall to another. The image was usually a picture painted onto a glass slide. The machine used to project the image was called a "magic lantern."

The images on the screen could be ghostly, comical, or spectacular. They might involve a moral lesson, teaching right and wrong. Some ghostly effects were achieved by projecting the image of a phantom onto smoke rather than a screen. This was all the more impressive when the magic lantern itself was kept out of sight.

Other subjects for these slide shows included a man swallowing rats, a clown performing, a naval battle, pottery-making, and a fantasy voyage beyond the moon. There was an illustrated lecture on the evils of alcohol. Some of these shows made extremely skillful use of **dissolves**. That is, they made one image fade into another in quick succession.

Dissolves began to create the illusion of movement. In a show about a famous fire in London, for example, the audience saw the smoke getting thicker and thicker. Then the flames grew higher and higher, and finally the fire died down as the firemen's hoses sprayed jets of water onto it.

The Challenge of Photography

At first, the slides used in magic lantern shows were hand painted. Circular, brightly colored pictures with lots of detail were painted by artists onto an area about $3\frac{1}{2}$ inches (90 mm) in diameter. Everything – the rigging on a ship, the leaves on a tree – could be clearly seen on the screen, even when magnified by a lens.

By the 1880s, hand-painted slides were being challenged by photographic slides. These were much cheaper to produce.

Left: Watching a magic lantern show.

The Magic Box

A camera has sometimes been called a "magic box." It is, of course, no more magic than a "magic" lantern. Both of them are based on a scientific understanding of the nature of light.

A Frenchman named Nicéphore Nièpce was the first person to succeed in taking a picture with a camera. The camera had a glass plate with light-sensitive chemicals on it. In 1826 he used it to fix an image of two houses side by side. It took eight hours.

Later developments soon reduced the necessary **exposure** time to between two and three seconds, in bright sunlight. But for sixty years, a heavy and breakable glass plate was the only type of base available to photographers. The exposure time, plus the heavy and fragile equipment, made early photography better suited to portraits and landscapes. It was difficult to capture anything in motion.

A photographer named Eadweard Muybridge was an exception to this. In 1872 the governor of California commissioned him to photograph his racehorses galloping. The governor wanted to settle a bet. He believed that at one point all four legs of a galloping horse are off the ground.

After five years, Muybridge proved the governor winner of the wager. He placed a long row of cameras side by side on the edge of a racetrack. The **shutter** of each camera was connected to a piece of thread stretched across the track. As the horse galloped past, it broke the threads. One by one, the shutter of each camera was released. The result was glass-plate photographs taken split seconds apart.

Film Speeds Up

In 1888, the Eastman company invented a flexible film on a roll. Within two years, it became possible to take up to 40 photographs a second.

Sharp-witted showmen soon became interested. They could see it was possible to make money out of the new invention. People were very willing to put coins into peepshow machines. These worked like a flip book. That is, they showed photographs at speeds fast enough to create the illusion of movement. These "movies" lasted less than a minute. They were watched by only one person at a time.

Business was good. But many people saw that it would be even better if a film could be projected for a large audience. The race was on.

Below: Muybridge's photographs of galloping horses helped the governor of California to win a bet.

The First Movies

It was this race to combine projection and photography that led up to the 1895 Paris film show. The winners were the Lumière brothers, Louis and Auguste. Working in their father's photographic factory, they put together a machine that could both expose film and project it. Made of mahogany and brass, it was called the *Lumière Cinematographe*.

Within two weeks of the Lumières' first public screening, scientists and showmen in other countries had also found a way of combining film and projection. As a result, the "movies," as they came to be called, spread across the United States and Europe within a year.

The First Documentaries
The first films offered to audiences were what we now call **documentaries**. The cameras, still heavy and difficult to move, were set up in one spot to film what was going on. The result was a typical Lumière show at the end of the century. It consisted of a collection of "shorts" such as *The Baby's First Lesson in Walking*, *The Fish Market at Marseilles*, *A Sack Race between Workers at the Lumière Factory*, and *German Dragoons Leaping the Hurdles*. To add to the enjoyment, this last item was shown backwards as well as forwards.

Right: Méliès' *Trip to the Moon* was the first big international success in movie history. Many more such trips followed.

Sometimes these films were livened up – for example, by attaching the camera to the top of a train. But it was some years before anyone tried out a totally different approach to film making.

Méliès – Movie Magician

The most successful of the early non-documentary film makers was Georges Méliès. Méliès had been a magician before becoming a moviemaker. He was interested in the film's ability to trick an audience. Méliès designed and built the world's first film studio. In 18 years he made over 1,000 movies. Some of them were short trick films, such as *The Man with the Rubber Head*. In it, Méliès himself plays an eccentric scientist who blows up his own head like a ballon, until it finally explodes.

He also made several 20-minute science fiction fantasies, based on the novels of Jules Verne. Of these, the most successful was *A Trip to the Moon*.

Bigger and Better

Having taken its first steps in the last years of the nineteenth century, film set out to conquer the world in the twentieth. Because they were silent, movies could be understood everywhere, not just in Europe and North America.

During World War I (1914–1918), movie production in Europe was interrupted. In the United States, however, it carried on. By 1920, Hollywood, California had become the movie capital of the world.

Many changes came to movies and motion picture equipment. Audiences had grown tired of short, silent, black-and-white movies. They wanted something bigger and better for their money.

The "Talkies"

People had been recording sound for more than 30 years before it was successfully added to motion pictures. Two problems had to be solved. The first was how to make the actors' speech (the dialogue) match their lip movements. The second was how to make the sound loud enough.

The Western Electric Company produced an answer in 1926. Warner Brothers bought their equipment and made *The Jazz Singer*. In it, the star, Al Jolson, had plenty of songs and a few lines of dialogue. Moviegoers loved it, and producers competed to bring out the first all-talking film. As a result of the coming of sound, audiences in the United States rose from 57 million a week in 1926 to 110 million in 1930.

Glorious Technicolor!

Color film, like sound, was possible for many years before the Technicolor system became generally accepted. The first Technicolor films used only two colors, red and green. The best known of these movies is *The Black Pirate*, made in 1926 by Douglas Fairbanks. The Technicolor film chemists did not stop there, and in six years they had worked out a way of adding blue.

Right: Jolson told audiences, "You ain't heard nothin' yet!"

Scope for Action

The novelty of sound and color began to wear off soon after World War II (1939–1945). And more important, the movies now had a powerful rival – television.

By the early 1950s, weekly movie ticket sales were down to around 50 million. Once again, the studio bosses demanded new ideas to bring back the audiences.

The Wide Screen

The most successful change made to movies in the 1950s was the introduction of CinemaScope. This system used a special kind of **lens** called **anamorphic** lens. When a movie is being shot, this lens "sees" a very wide area of action. It squeezes the image onto ordinary 35-mm film. Later, an anamorphic lens, turned the other way around, is fitted to the projector. It stretches out the image so that it regains its original shape when it reaches the screen.

CinemaScope was relative-

Below and left: These scenes from *The Robe* show how much more action can be packed onto a CinemaScope screen compared to a standard screen.

——— STANDARD SCREEN

— CINEMASCOPE

ly cheap to use because it did not require a new type of film or camera. But it did require a much wider screen than the one in use at the time.

To make the best use of this new invention, movies were made with plenty of action and dazzling spectacle. *The Robe*, a Biblical epic, was the first.

"A Lion in your Lap!"

Another idea was developed in the 1950s. It was three-dimensional film, known as 3-D. This attempted to give the picture on the screen depth as well as height and width.

Above: This publicity poster gives a rather optimistic impression of 3-D.

To show a 3-D movie, two separate projectors had to be used at the same time. One showed red images, the other showed green. The audience had to wear special glasses, with one red lens and one green lens. In return, they mostly got things hurled at them, or monsters jumping out at them. When the novelty wore off, 3-D was more or less abandoned. It made a small-scale comeback in the 1980s, with *Jaws 3-D*.

23

Cinerama

Many other new movie techniques were tried out in the 1950s. One was Cinerama. It claimed to bring "total reality" to the experience of watching a movie.

Cinerama was based on the fact that our eyes give us a curved view of the world around us. This sweeping arc is about 150 degrees wide and 50 degrees high. The Cinerama system tried to achieve the same effect. It used three cameras, all on the same stand, for shooting the film, and three projectors for showing it.

Cinerama required a gigantic screen, about 30 feet (9 m) high and 90 feet (27 m) long. It was curved, and practically surrounded the front rows of the movie theater. One projector was placed, as usual, in the center. Another, on the right side of the theater, projected its image onto the left curve. The third projector beamed its image at the right curve. The three separate beams joined up as a single picture on the screen.

Cinerama was mostly used to make movies that could show off the new system. For example, audiences of *This is Cinerama* found themselves in the front seat of a roller

coaster. Some people actually felt queasy at the end of their "ride." In the early 1960s a few Cinerama features were made. But they were expensive to produce, and the use of Cinerama soon died out.

Smell-o-Vision and Sensurround

Two other movie novelties were Smell-o-Vision and, years later, Sensurround.

To make Smell-o-Vision work, individual odor outlets were installed for each seat in the movie theater. Electronic signals on the "smell-track" of the film triggered

the release of the odors.

Scent of Mystery was one movie made in Smell-o-Vision. Audiences watching it received whiffs of over 30 different odors that linked up with the action on the screen. Among these were shoe polish, pipe tobacco, bread being baked, a salty ocean breeze, garlic, carnations, peppermint, coffee, lavender, gunsmoke, and fresh air.

Sensurround tried out the idea of giving the audience something to feel, as well as see and hear. When Los Angeles began to break up in the film *Earthquake*, the audience felt themselves being shaken all over. The effect was produced by

Above: Audiences reacted favorably to Smell-o-Vision and enjoyed being rattled around by Sensurround. Both ideas were short-lived, however.

powerful loudspeakers at the front and back of the theater. Each gave out a low-pitched rumbling sound.

70-mm Film

One further development worth mentioning is 70-mm film. Twice as wide as standard 35-mm film, it is expensive. But it can produce a bigger, sharper image and better quality sound. It is used quite often today.

Movies of the Future

In the late 1960s, the IMAX system was invented in Canada. It produces the largest film image ever seen. A typical IMAX screen is 45 feet (14 m) high and 62 feet (19 m) wide. The floor of the theater is very steep, so that each row of seats is about two feet higher than the row in front. This gives every member of the audience a perfect view of the screen.

IMAX uses ordinary film to fill this huge screen. But it does so in an unusual way. It takes 70-mm film and runs it through the camera from left to right, rather than from top to bottom. It is later run through the projector in the same way.

As a result, 70-mm becomes the *height* of the frame rather than the *width*. This makes an IMAX frame the largest ever used. It is just over 5 square inches (32 square cm) in area. This is ten times larger than the frame on 35-mm film.

Because the image is so large and so clear, the audience can "experience" it rather than just watch it. The curved screen is so high and wide that the audience is not really aware of its edges. To add to this, the soundtrack comes from huge speakers placed in different parts of the theater. The sound surrounds the audience instead of simply coming from the front. Audience involvement can be total.

So far, the movies made using the IMAX system have concentrated on traveling and scenery. One of them is called simply *To Fly*. It shows views from balloons, vintage aircraft, helicopters, stunt planes, jets, and hang gliders.

The IMAX system is, however, very expensive to install. Also, no one has yet

Left: An IMAX screen is vast, but the auditorium seats relatively few people. Showing here is *To Fly*.

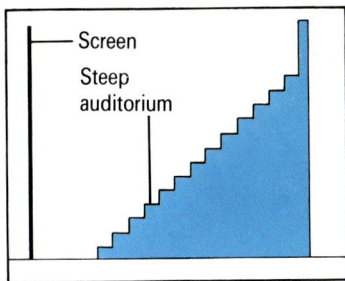

Above: The steep IMAX auditorium raises each row above the one in front, so that everyone can see perfectly.

worked out a way of filming a full-length entertainment feature with it.

Showscan

Another new process is called Showscan. It, too, aims to involve the audience more. So far, it has only been used in the United States. Showscan uses a screen that is slightly curved, like Cinerama. It is wide, like CinemaScope. The film is 70-mm.

What makes Showscan different is its frame rate. It is photographed and projected at 60 frames per second. This is $2\frac{1}{2}$ times faster than the standard rate. The result, its inventor claims, is picture quality better than anything ever seen before.

Like IMAX, Showscan theaters have a steeply angled floor, with only 100 seats.

Picture Palaces

During the last years of the 1800s, the early movies were fairly short. They were usually just one part of a varied program of entertainment. But it was soon clear that the public was willing to pay just to see movies. Local stores and halls began to be converted into movie theaters..

On the average, there would be about fifteen shows a day. The seats were just ordinary wooden chairs, but the audiences still kept coming. From about 1905, movie theaters were specially designed and built. The programs became longer,

and the seats more comfortable.

An Escape into Adventure
The great age of movie theater building came after World War I. In large cities, some of these could seat several thousand people.

Many movie theaters were elaborately decorated. Their palace-like interiors offered audiences an escape from the rather drab postwar world. Some were decorated to look like Chinese pagodas, while others copied Egyptian temples or Spanish villas. Some had exotic names, such as the

Alhambra and the *Trocadero*. Inside were marble staircases, glittering chandeliers, and mosaic floors. Splendidly uniformed ushers led customers to plushly padded seats. The best movie theaters also had a restaurant. A full-time professional organist played background music before the program began.

A New Approach
In the 1950s and 1960s movie audiences began to diminish. Theaters were forced to close down as fast as they had been put up 30 years before.

A new way of presenting movies has met with success in the United States and is being adopted in Europe. It is called a "multiplex." This goes back to the old idea of making the movie just one of many attractions offered.

Below: Drive-in movies, where audiences watch from their cars, continue to be popular in the United States.

Making a Feature of It

To make a feature film, somebody first has to have an idea. If enough investors think the idea is a good one, then the movie gets financial "backing." It usually takes one or two years for the idea to become a finished movie. But in some cases this period may be much longer, or much shorter.

One of the most common film ideas is the "movie from the book." From Méliès to the present day, moviemakers have frequently taken books, old and new, as their starting point. The more famous the book, the more likely it is to be filmed. The Bible, for example, has provided stories for countless films, such as the *Ten Commandments*. The plays of Shakespeare have been filmed in many languages. Other famous books brought to the big screen include *The Wizard of Oz*, *Lord of the Rings*, *The Jungle Book*, *A Passage to India*, and *The Little Prince*.

Successful stage shows have also been frequently taken as the basis for a film. *Oklahoma*, *West Side Story*, *Grease*, and *Oliver!* all became films in this way.

Sequels and Quickies

If a film is popular, then producers will often consider making a **sequel**. The sequel is based on the same characters and situations as the original film. Many recent sequels have simply added a number to the original title – for example, *Rocky 3*.

Another kind of production idea is the "quickie." Here producers try and cash in on a fashion quickly, while it lasts. *Breakdance* and *BMX Bandits* were two recent quickies. *Breakdance* was planned in January, 1984. Shooting began in February. The editing was done in April, and by early May the film was being screened all over the United States. It made so much money at the box office that the producers instantly produced a sequel called *Breakdance 2*.

Right: The hero is back. *Indiana Jones and the Temple of Doom* **successfully** **repeated the thrill-a-minute formula of *Raiders of the Lost Ark*.**

Credit Where It's Due

At the beginning and the end of a movie, the **credits** are shown. These give information on who has done what in the making of the movie. They show very clearly that moviemaking is always the result of teamwork.

Besides the stars, the most important names to appear before the movie starts are those of the producer and the director. The producer has overall control, and looks after the money budgeted for the movie. The director is in charge of the creative side of the movie.

Once the idea for the movie has been agreed upon, the

producer has to work out what it is likely to cost. Then the idea has to be sold to someone with enough money to invest. Another job is finding the best writer and director for the subject. While the movie is actually being filmed, the production team also keeps an eye on the day-to-day spending.

One of the director's main jobs is **casting** the right actors for the movie. His primary concern is getting the best performance out of each actor. But even a brilliant performance is wasted if it is poorly filmed. So the director is also concerned with lighting, cameras, and other technical aspects. There are often two or three assistant directors to help – especially when crowds of **extras** are involved.

Key to picture:
1 Lights on rail
2 Painted backdrop
3 Fan blowing plastic snow
4 Script supervisor
5 Microphone operator
6 Microphone boom
7 Smoke/fog machine
8 Director
9 Light
10 Camera crew
11 Second assistant cameraman

Getting the Look Right

Louis Lumière invented the *Cinematographe* over 90 years ago. That term is still important in moviemaking today. **Cinematographer** is now the name given to the person who is responsible for the overall "look" of the film as the public will see it.

At its simplest, this means that he or she has to make sure that the filming is done for the most effective result. The audience must be able to understand and get the most out of what it sees on the screen. This involves controlling the choice of film, camera lens, camera angle, and sources of light.

The audience is not always meant to notice the work that goes into cinematography. It often just means that the film is easy to watch. At other times, a dramatic use of shadows, or of a **deep-focus** lens, deliberately adds meaning to a shot.

Makeup

Another person concerned with the "look" is the makeup artist. Over the years, makeup artists have developed many materials to help them in their job. These include wax, plastic, foam, greasepaint, resin, spirit gum, hair, rubber, and even special lenses for the eyes.

Every movie uses makeup to some extent. Some would be impossible to make without it. In such movies as *Citizen Kane* and *Little Big Man*, the makeup artist had to be able to age the actors by 50 years or more. Other movies, such as *Frankenstein* and *Star Wars*, needed convincing "monster" makeup. In *Planet of the Apes*, all of the main actors except one wore ape makeup throughout the movie. It took five hours each day for each actor to apply and remove the ape mask.

Makeup doesn't just mean shaping a new face for an actor. Sometimes it involves designing and making a complete outfit. The gillman in *The Creature from the Black Lagoon* and the apes in *Greystoke* were created in this way.

The importance of good makeup artists has only recently been recognized. They can now win Oscars. The first Oscar for makeup went to Rick Baker, for his work on *An American Werewolf in London*, in 1982.

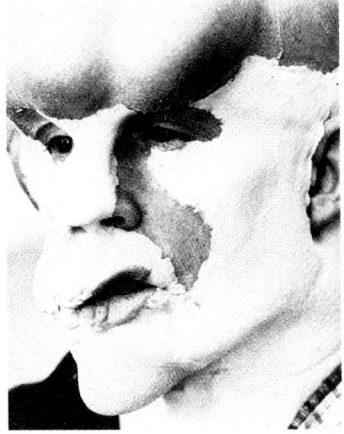

Making up John Hurt to look like *The Elephant Man* was a lengthy and complicated job. The makeup consisted of fifteen separate sections, with each piece overlapping some of the others. It took eight weeks to work it out, and then eight hours each day to put it on. It was extremely uncomfortable to wear. The actor and makeup artist, Chris Tucker, had to start work at four in the morning, so that shooting could begin at midday.

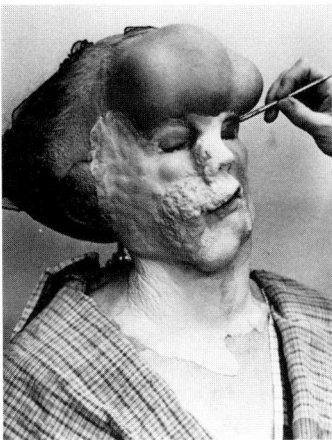

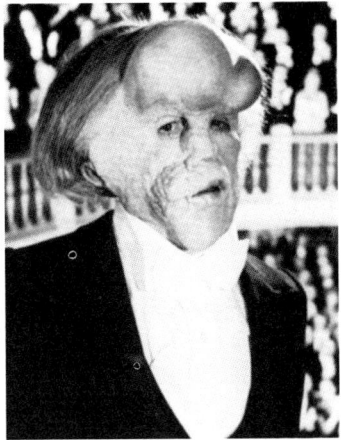

Stunting

Many of the exciting fights and chase scenes in the movies would be impossible to create without the help of stunt **doubles**. Yet it is only since the 1970s that their names have begun to appear in the credits.

Risky Business

In the days of silent movies, stars were usually expected to do all their own stunts, however dangerous. Pearl White, who played the heroine in *The Perils of Pauline*, had to climb up the outside of a tall building. She also had to be thrown off a cliff and battle with various savage animals. In one such scene, she seriously injured her back.

When that kind of thing happened to a star, it was expensive for the studio. As a result, stars no longer were allowed to do their own stunts, and doubles took over.

Stunt doubles soon became adept at doing "transfer" stunts, as well as falls and fights. They transferred at high speed from a motorcycle to an airplane, or from a car to a train, or from a horse to a stagecoach.

This last stunt was performed in many films by one of the pioneer stunt doubles, Yakima Canutt. Standing in for the hero, he would ride after a stagecoach going at full speed. Having brought his horse alongside, he would gradually haul himself up to the top. There he would fight furiously with the escaping "bad guy." As if this wasn't

enough, he would then be knocked off the stagecoach, falling among the galloping hooves. Letting the coach pass over him, he would grab the rear axle. Finally, he would climb back up on top to take his opponent by surprise. Yet Canutt's name never appeared in the credits.

The more recent *Raiders of the Lost Ark* carefully re-created this stunt, using a truck instead of a stage-coach. But today, stunt doubles are usually given credit for their work. There was no attempt to pretend that Harrison Ford, the star, had done this dangerous part himself.

Modern technology has produced air bags which cushion a fall without causing a dangerous rebound. Even so, stunting remains a risky job.

Below: Mattresses break the fall for this group of Mexican stuntmen.

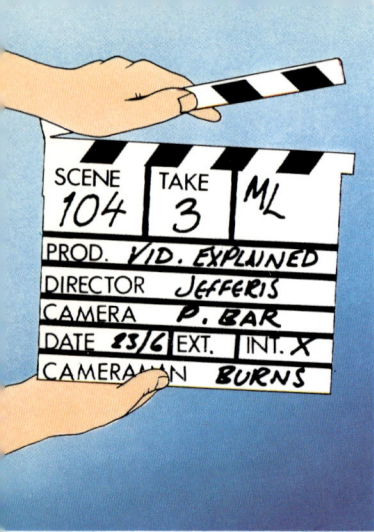

Left: The clapper board consists of two hinged pieces of wood that are brought together sharply at the start of each take. This helps the director and editor to keep the takes in order.

Film critics enjoy spotting continuity blunders. For example, during one musical number in *The King and I*, Yul Brynner can be seen wearing an earring in some shots – but not in others. In *Anatomy of a Murder*, Lee Remick is seen in a restaurant wearing a dress. When she walks outside, she is suddenly wearing slacks.

Behind the Screen

Hundreds of other people are involved in the making of a movie. Some of them get a credit, some of them don't.

The script supervisor certainly hopes that his or her work *won't* be noticed by the audience. If it is noticed, then it must have been done badly. This job involves making sure that each shot in the finished film flows smoothly into the next shot. There should be no changes of detail unless they are part of the storyline. This can be tricky, because the different scenes in a movie are not shot in order.

Sound and Vision

At least five people usually back up the camera operator. One is the first assistant cameraman. His or her main job is to keep the camera in **focus** and to change the lens when necessary.

At the other end of the camera, the film has to be loaded and taken out. The person who does this is also in charge of the clapper-board.

In the credits this job is usually shown as second assistant cameraman.

The gaffer is the chief electrician. He or she works to get the lighting effects required by the cinematographer. As head of the grip department, the key grip ensures smooth camera **tracking** and provides support to the electrical department. Grips are often in charge of other rigging on a set. Finally, best boys assist both the gaffer and key grip.

Recording the sound track is also a team effort. On the set are the boom operator and the sound mixer. The boom is a long, adjustable rod with a microphone on the end of it. The operator moves the boom as necessary to pick up dialogue and other live sound.

Later, when shooting is over, the final soundtrack is put together by the sound editor. There are usually music tracks and sound effects tracks to add to the dialogue tracks. These have to be blended smoothly by the sound mixer into a single track.

Below: *Supergirl*, filmed at Pinewood studios in England, employed one engineering shop, two model workshops and a mechanical special effects unit.

Selling the Movie

Between the making of a movie and screening it, there is a process called **distribution**. The distributor aims to get the movie seen by as large an audience as possible. In return, the distributor gets a fee or a percentage of the profits that the movie will make.

One of the first things a distributor does is voluntarily submit the movie to the Motion Picture Association of America for rating. There, a board consisting of six parents watches the film and decides for what age level it is suitable.

After consideration, the board issues a rating – "G (General)," "PG (Parental Guidance)," "PG 13," "R (Restricted)," or "X." Sometimes scenes are cut in order to get a different rating. *Footloose*, for example, would have been rated PG 13, but a violent scene was cut so that the board would agree to a PG rating. This made it available to a much wider audience.

Another part of the distributor's job is to work out how many prints of the movie are gong to be needed. Each print costs around $1,400 to make. Some audiences will either want to see movies immediately or not at all. For such movies a "blanket" release is planned. This means that enough prints have to be made for the film to be shown all over the country at the same time. For

Below: An attention-grabbing poster helps to sell the movie to the public.

a new James Bond movie, more than a thousand prints may be made at the same time for release in the United States.

Finally, before the movie opens to the public, the distributor organizes a publicity campaign. Some of this, such as posters and advertising, is very expensive. The distributor will also try to get free publicity by persuading TV and radio producers to invite one of the stars onto a talk show.

Often, a song is written specifically to accompany and promote a movie. A popular song can reach millions of people daily by radio. The record and movie of *Ghostbusters* illustrate this very well.

How does Eddie Murphy follow a movie like Trading Places?

Easy

BEVERLY HILLS
Cop

15

Going to the Movies

Going to the movies is quite a different experience from watching the same film on TV. The picture, of course, is larger and clearer. But more than this, sharing a film with the other members of the audience can be a big part of the enjoyment. A comedy seems much funnier when a group of people laugh at it together. A thriller becomes more thrilling. Even a horror movie may be more fun to watch when the audience can give each other a sense of security.

Ever since the early days of moviegoing, the sale of food and drink has always been important. People like to eat when they go to the movies, whether they are hungry or not! Movie theaters depend more on the profits from the sale of candy, ice cream, hot dogs, popcorn, and beverages than they do on the sale of admission tickets.

Showing the Movie

Inside the movie theater, the film is prepared and shown by the projectionist. He or she works in a room above

Above: Going to the movies involves more than just the feature film.

and behind the audience. When a 35-mm feature arrives at a theater, it is in five or six separate cans. Each can contains 2,000 feet (610 m) of film, which will give 20 minutes of screen time. Very often the movie is gong to be shown in the same theater for at least a week. If so, the projectionist will normally **splice** all the reels together, end to end. Then the whole thing is transferred onto one enormous spool. This way only one

projector is needed and the film can be left to run on its own.

If the movie is only going to be shown once or twice, the projectionist keeps the reels separate. Two projectors are used to keep the film going without a break. A small black dot, printed in the top right-hand corner of the film near the end of the reel, tells the projectionist when to get the second projector started. The dot appears on the screen for four frames; that is, one-sixth of a second.

If the projectionist doesn't notice the dot, there will be a break in the action between one reel and the next. Audiences may complain, their concentration and enjoyment spoiled.

Just about as annoying is the showing of a poor-quality print. Film is delicate and damages easily. Color film can fade with age even when handled carefully, film gets battered and strained by projection. One flaw in a projector can scratch every film that runs through it. Good projectionists do what they can to clean up and mend the prints they show. But scratches just won't go away.

Along Came Video

Television and video are usually thought of as being very modern. They are actually only 30 years younger than the movies. In the 1920s, the British inventor John Logie Baird worked on both ideas, with some success. He gave a public demonstration of television in 1928 by transmitting a picture from London to New York City using electronic signals.

At the same time, Baird developed a brittle plastic video-disc. It worked in the same way as a phonograph record. This disc fitted onto a turntable which revolved 78 times per minute. When the needle came into contact with the disc, electronic signals were sent to a TV receiver to which it was connected. A visual image appeared. The disc produced 12 still images, each of which stayed on the screen for about 15 seconds.

TV and Video

For a few years these discs were on sale to the general public. However, the possibilities of video were not fully explored for another twenty years.

The idea was revived in the 1950s. This time the demand came from television companies. In those days, every program had to be either transmitted live, mistakes and all, or recorded on film, which was very expensive. An inexpensive recording system was urgently needed.

The answer came in 1956. An American company called Ampex produced a system using tape rather than discs.

Above: A picture produced on a receiver by one of Baird's video disks in 1938. It lasted several seconds.

Videotape works in exactly the same way as audio tapes (the tapes we listen to). Both are made from plastic film. The film is coated with a layer of magnetic particles. If the tape is passed over a **recording head**, the electric signals from the head change the pattern of the particles. When the tape is played back at the same speed, the recording head "reads" the magnetic pattern. So the electronic signals reproduce the original sound and picture it recorded.

But much more information needs to be stored on a videotape than when simply recording sound. The Ampex equipment solved this problem by using 2-inch wide (5-cm) tape. It used four recording heads instead of one. Furthermore, each of the heads rotated while the tape passed over it. The system produced exellent playback quality.

Good though the Ampex system was, there was room for improvement. The equipment was expensive and heavy. Each machine was about 10 feet (3 m) high, 6 feet (2 m) wide, and 3 feet (1 m) deep. The spools were up to $4\frac{1}{2}$ feet (1.5 m) wide. A system that used narrower tape was needed. Once the tape was

Below: A modern Laser-Vision disk. It spins at 18,000 revolutions per minute, and contains 108,000 frames.

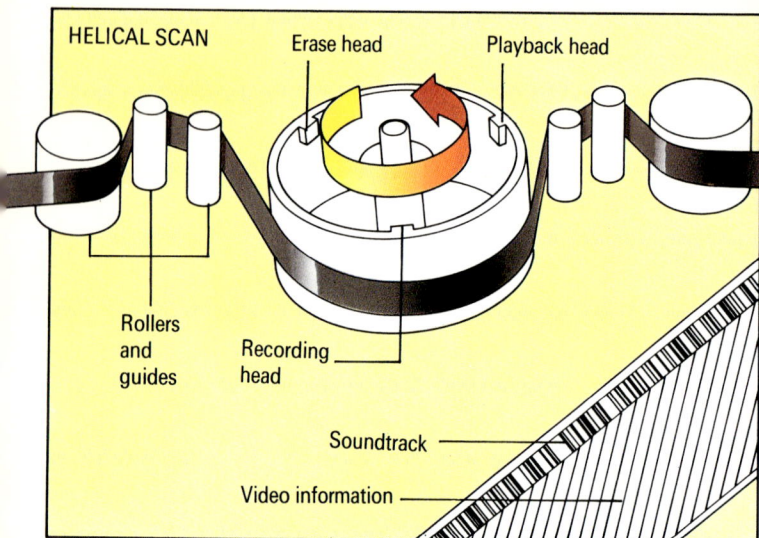

HELICAL SCAN

Erase head

Playback head

Rollers
and
guides

Recording
head

Soundtrack

Video information

narrower, the rest of the equipment could be scaled down, too.

In 1964 the lead was taken by the Japanese company Toshiba. They developed a technique that was originally known as "slant back" recording. This name describes it very well. What it means is that the tape passes over the head at a slant, not at a right angle. All the information is laid down in long, slanting tracks. In this way 2-inches (5 cm) worth of pictures can be packed onto tape only 1 inch (2.5 cm) wide. The sound is recorded by a separate recording head. It is laid down on one edge of the tape.

The **slant track** system came to be known as the **helical scan** system. At first it worked by having the **supply spool** mounted higher than the **takeup spool**, with the recording head in the middle. The tape then had to pass over the head.

Later, tape became even narrower, and small video machines were introduced for use in the home. In these machines, helical scan was achieved by having the head drum leaning over to one side. If you take the cassette out of a home video (VCR) and shine a flashlight inside, you should be able to see the leaning drum.

Video in TV

The video breakthrough of 1956 completely changed television broadcasting. Suddenly, things which had been impossible became easy. As a result, it is fairly rare to see a "live" broadcast on TV these days.

Playback and Editing

Weekly sports coverage would seem to be an obvious example of live television. But even in these programs video is used a great deal. Prerecorded interviews and slow-motion action replays from different angles would be impossible without video. A live event such as the launch of a space shuttle is recorded on video as it goes out. Later it will be played back as an **edited** news item.

Video also made possible the editing of television programs. In the days when most programs went out live, studio plays, quiz shows, and comedy shows often contained a variety of mistakes and blunders. Many overran

Below: Electronic News Gathering is one of video's latest conquests over film.

their time and had to be cut off before the end. Now, prerecording and editing make them mistake-free and exactly the right length.

Out and About
The last area of television to be affected by video was the news. Even after helical scanning was invented, video recording equipment was still too bulky and heavy to be moved around easily. Trucks with cameras and recording equipment were able to cover some news events, but not all of them. They could only go where there were roads.

During the 1950s and 1960s, television had to rely on film more than on video for recording unscheduled

---

AN OUTSIDE BROADCAST VAN

1 Power supply
2 Production desk
3 Monitor
4 Twin videotape recorders

5 Other equipment
6 Air conditioning
7 Camera operator
8 Engineer's desk

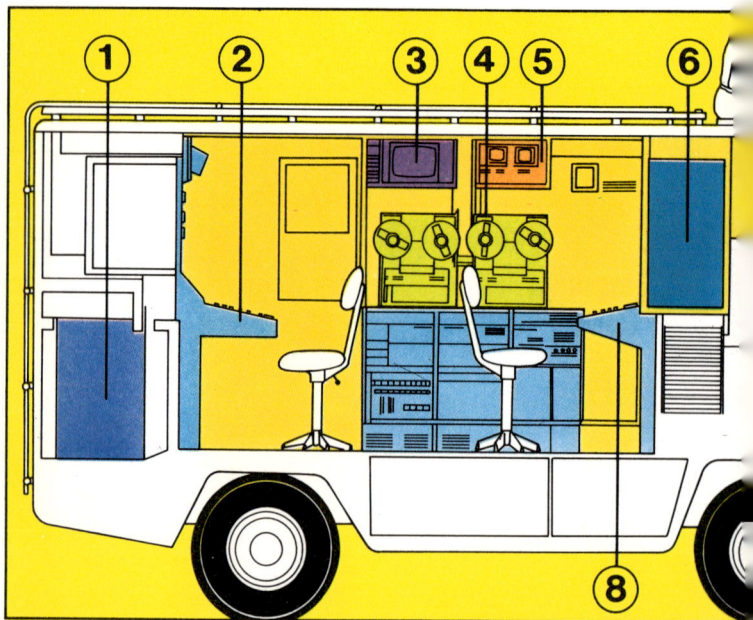

news events. Film cameras, being portable, could reach places video cameras could not get near. However there was a big disadvantage. The film had to by physically carried back to the studio, and chemically processed. This resulted in a delay of several hours before it could be shown on television.

In the 1970s all this changed. The Japanese Sony company invented the U-Matic video format. This used tape only $\frac{3}{4}$ of an inch (2 cm) wide, inside a cassette. It could be used with a lightweight camera. U-Matic video recording soon took over from film. This system is now known as ENG (electronic news gathering). It does not need to be either processed or transported. Instead, it is electronically transmitted back to the studio (or sent by satellite from one country to another) within seconds. ENG is also cheaper, because it needs fewer operators than film.

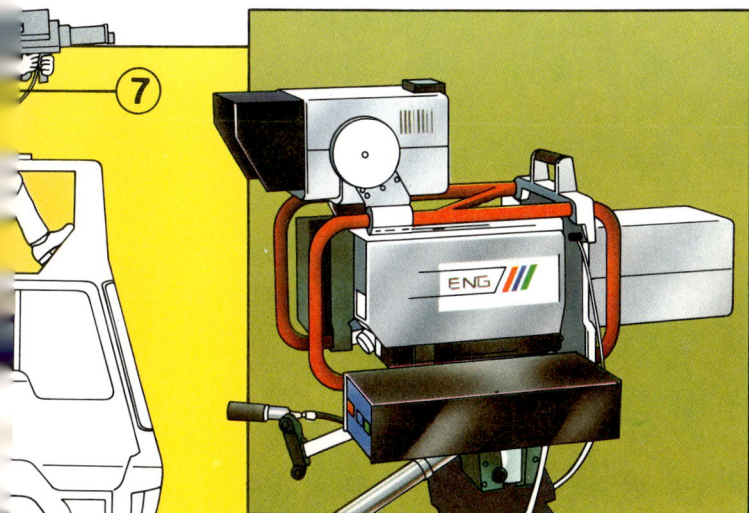

Above: An ENG camera is so light that one operator, with an assistant, can take it anywhere.

Rock Videos

Most rock videos make use of both film and video.

Often, the ideas for the video are first **storyboarded**. Then they are shot onto 35-mm film. Everything is shot several times. Each time different camera angles, backgrounds, lighting, and performances are used. This will probably use up around one hour of film. The film will then have to be edited down to about three minutes, to fit the song.

One way of doing this is to copy it from film onto videotape. This process is known as **telecine transfer**. Using a video editing suite, the job of cutting and rearranging the material can be done quickly and cleanly.

Special Powers

Once the video has been edited, other **post-production** work can be done on it.

A good example is the work done on the video for Michael Jackson's record **Billie Jean**. The video was based on the idea of Jackson having special powers. Paving slabs were made to light up as he stepped on them. Figures in advertisements became animated, in time

with his singing. Special effects such as these are usually added at post-production stage.

Most videos are made in a few days, at a cost of around $30,000. A few superstars, however, have spent more money in an attempt to produce something extra-special. The longest, most ambitious, and most expensive video yet made is

Michael Jackson's *Thriller*. Unlike most videos, this was not produced quickly just to help sell a record. The song was already world-famous before the video was made.

Jackson hired a top director, top makeup artist and top dance arranger to work with him on the project. He chose John Landis to direct, and Rick Baker to do the makeup. He had seen and admired their work on the movie *An American Werewolf in London*. The new techniques of **animatronics** (described in chapter 7) were used, as well as makeup and masks, to transform him into a man-panther. The result, shot and edited on film, lasted 14 minutes and cost one million dollars. The video has played in some movie theaters as a short subject. It has also won fame as a video.

Below: Jackson's *Thriller* – not so much a promotion film as a mini-movie.

Powerful Promotion

Nearly 3,000 rock videos are now made each year. About 1,500 of these are made in the United States.

Record companies try to outdo one another with the videos they produce. They hope that each video will be packed with enough originality and technical brilliance to make a lasting impact. This is because the aim of most rock videos is to promote and sell the record they accompany. Most of all, producers want their videos to be played on MTV, the nonstop rock video TV channel.

Video in the Clubs

Television is not the only possible outlet for rock videos. In some nightclubs around the country there are now "video jukeboxes." By putting money into a slot, customers can select a video, which is then played automatically. Discos are another outlet for videos as well as records. This could mean that DJs will be gradually replaced by VJs.

Below: The futuristic fantasy of Duran Duran's award-winning _Wild Boys_ video.

Video in Moviemaking

Moviemaking is another area where film and video sometimes work side by side. Movie producers are always eager to cut costs. Where video offers a way of saving time and money, they are likely to use it.

Instant Rushes

For over 60 years, a movie director's working day has involved watching the **rushes**. These are the prints made from the filming done the day before. The director has to be satisfied that some of the **takes** are good enough for the final print. Sometimes none of the takes have worked very well. If this happens, then the director has to restage and reshoot the entire scene. Setting everything up again is a costly business.

To avoid the extra cost, directors working on big productions record on film and video at the same time. The director can check the video within minutes of a scene being staged and filmed. He or she can decide whether the film take is going to be satisfactory when printed. If it is not, then the scene can be reshot right away, while everything is set up.

Sometimes a particular effect has to be added to a film at a later stage. Video can be useful here. In *The Company of Wolves*, for example, the script called for a wolf's head to be chopped off. This action was to be shown in slow motion. Video was used by the film unit to check

Right: Shooting on video provides instant "rushes" for the director's guidance.

on whether their head-chopping sequence was going to look effective when slowed down.

Feedback for Monsters

There is another way in which the small screen can help out the big screen. This happens in moviemaking when people have to operate puppets or monsters, or other non-humans. During the filming of *The Dark Crystal*, the puppeteers operating characters called Jen and Kira were hidden below the stage. In order to see their own hands "acting," and to avoid bumping into each other, the puppeteers had small TV screens showing them live pictures from the stage.

Similarly, in *Return to Oz*, there was an actor inside Tik-Tok, a character made up mainly of a large metal sphere. The actor had to walk backwards, bent over double, during the action. In order to see where he was going, he had a tiny TV inside his costume.

Below: Using a telecine transfer unit, programs shot on film may be transferred to video for ease of playback.

Video Comes Home

Above: Annual VCR sales have exceeded that of radios, music centers and washing machines in many countries.

Video has only recently become inexpensive and convenient enough for use in the home. As early as 1964, Toshiba brought out a $\frac{1}{2}$-inch (1.3-cm) system for home use, but it never became very popular. It was based on the reel-to-reel system. This meant that people had to handle the tape themselves and thread it through a fairly tricky path on a slant.

Home video successfully arrived in the mid-70's. First, Sony introduced its $\frac{1}{2}$-inch Betamax system. Like the U-Matic, the tape was enclosed in a cassette and slipped easily into the recorder. It was no longer necessary for the user to touch the tape at all. Soon, a similar video home system (VHS) was on the market. There are more companies producing VHS equipment than the BETA tape format. VHS uses a larger cassette and has a longer playing time.

By 1985 nearly 34 percent of the homes in North America had a video system. Within the same 10 years, 45 percent of homes in Britain had video. In France the figure is around 17 percent.

Most videocassette recorders (VCRs) have a timer device. This feature has made VCR very popular for home use. Programs can be recorded if they are on at an inconvenient time. Some VCRs can be programmed for up to two weeks. This way, you won't miss your favorite soap opera while on vacation! A tape recording can then be played back anytime. Sometimes it is desirable to watch two programs being transmitted at the same time. One can simply be recorded while watching the other.

Prerecorded videocassettes are now available from thousands of local outlets. You can rent a videocassette

Below: Inside a video-cassette recorder.

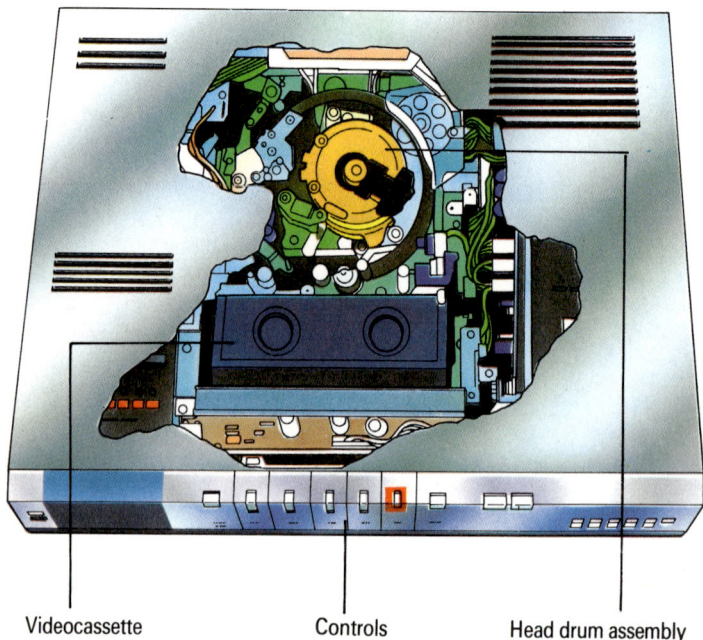

Videocassette   Controls   Head drum assembly

Case top
and flap

Twin spool
and tape

Lower
half of
case

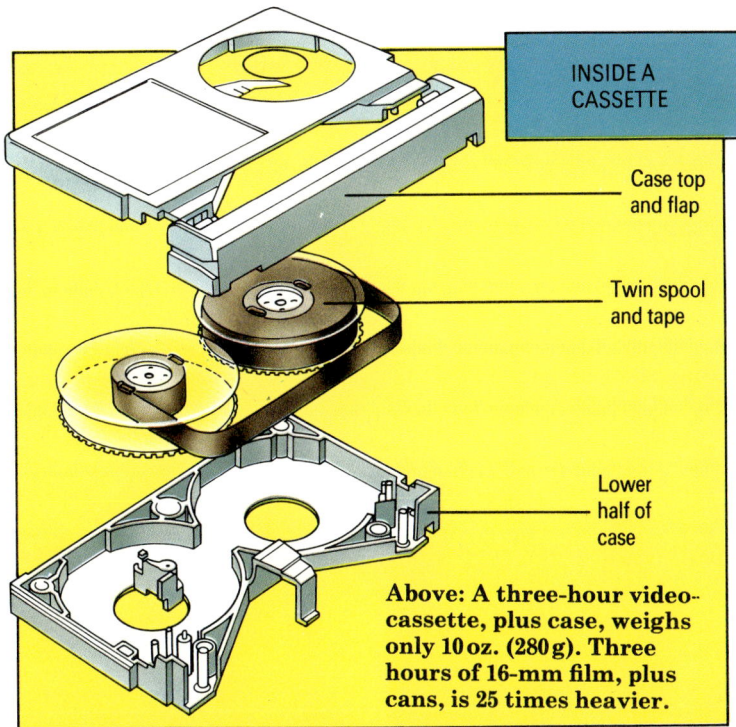

Above: A three-hour video-cassette, plus case, weighs only 10 oz. (280 g). Three hours of 16-mm film, plus cans, is 25 times heavier.

overnight, or longer if you wish, for only a few dollars.

At first, the only type of material available on video-cassettes were full-length features. New movies may be available on video within a year of their original release.

Now there is a much greater range of videos available. They can be purchased or rented. There are all sorts of how-to-do-it tapes. For sports fans, there are tapes about diving, tennis, wind-surfing, squash, and many others. For example, if you want to study closely how someone serves in tennis, then the replay and **freeze-frame** facilities on a VCR can be very useful.

Other tapes include cooking lessons, learning a foreign language, fitness exercises, self-defense, yoga, passing a driving test, dog training, pottery, studying for exams, and growing vegetables.

You can now even borrow cassettes from some local libraries in the same way that you borrow books.

The Video World

Video is an established part of TV and the movies. Today it is spreading into many other areas of life. Video can be used to inform and educate in schools, offices, hospitals, and stores. Progress has been so rapid that many new ideas, such as video telephones, may soon become a reality.

In many supermarkets and other stores, you are likely to see signs that say, "Video recording is in operation in this store." Cameras constantly survey shoppers as they take goods from the shelves. If store detectives suspect someone of stealing, video may provide evidence.

Video can help catch bank robbers, too. In the event of a robbery, a bank teller can set off a video camera simply by touching a foot switch.

Video Training

Many professionals – sales personnel, teachers, gymnasts, actors – can improve

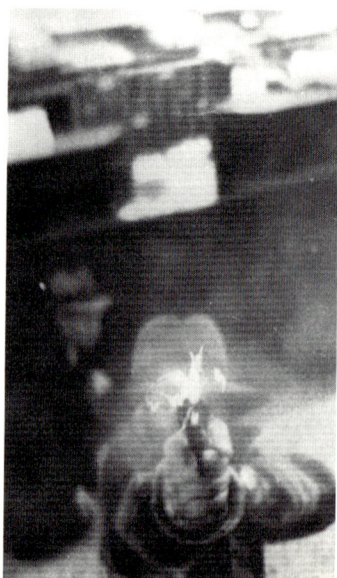

their performance by the use of video recordings.

Some fire departments now use videos to make an on-the-spot record of fires. The recording shows how each fire was managed. Such videotapes are later used for training purposes. New recruits can learn a lot about firefighting just from watching the videos.

Supermarket and department store staffs are often shown specially-made videos on topics related to the work they will be doing. Training managers find that these tapes help new employees far more than lectures used to.

In some cases, people can benefit from watching themselves in action. A gymnast or fencer, for example, may want to study his or her movements and work on improving them. Slow-motion video is very helpful here.

The Giant Screen

Video and TV are no longer confined to small, indoor screens. Since 1980, they have also moved onto giant screens. The image is bright and easily seen, even in glaring sunlight.

This system was pioneered by the Mitsubishi Corporation in Japan. A home TV set uses just one **electron beam tube**. Mitsubishi's Diamond-Vision screen may contain as many as 150,000 tubes. These give out such brightness that it is best for a viewer to be at least 150 feet (50 m) away.

The size and shape of these screens varies according to what sort of pictures are going to be shown on them. For team sports such as baseball, football, or soccer, screens of about 25 feet (8 m) high and 30 feet (10 m) wide are common. Horseracing, however, requires a screen shaped more like "Cinema-Scope."

The images shown on the screen can come from a number of sources. Most

Above: Top rock musicians often play in huge stadiums. Without the giant screen, must fans would hardly be able to see the stage.

event. Before a game starts there may be taped interviews with some of the players. There may be recorded highlights from some previous games. During the game itself, video can be used to provide action replay of exciting moments – as in TV broadcasts.

Video Concerts

Sports events are not the only users of giant screens. In 1985 Live Aid concerts took place at the same time in Philadelphia and London, England. Both had Diamond-Vision screens inside the huge stadiums. Without them, thousands of people in the audience wouldn't have been able to see anything at all. Live pictures were also beamed by satellite from the London stage to the Philadelphia screen, and vice versa.

At a rock concert, unlike a sporting event, the action is more or less fixed in one place – the stage. The camera operators can be positioned very close to the band. Some may be just below the level of the stage. Also, ENG equipment is so light that operators can move around the stage itself. They can get side-views and rear-views of the performance.

come live from ENG cameras operated within the stadium itself. For a sports event, the cameras obviously have to keep out of the way of the action. So the camera operators usually work from a distance.

Prerecorded videotapes can also be used for extra entertainment at a sports

The Video Watchdog

Video has given the police a powerful tool. Their cameras are used as part of a closed-circuit television (CCTV) setup. This means that the cameras transmit pictures which can be watched live in a control room. Later, if necessary, the police can watch the pictures again on video.

Police use CCTV regularly at events that attract large crowds. The cameras, operated by **remote control**, are constantly on the lookout for trouble. In this way, one person watching several screens in the control room can survey the whole scene. The cameras, being high up, can see a lot more than officers on the ground can.

Zooming In

If one of the screens shows a troublespot, a camera lens zooms in for a closer look. If necessary, police officers mingling with crowds are contacted by radio. If an arrest has to be made, the video recording can later be shown in court as evidence.

Because of this possibility, all police video cameras are fitted with a special mechanism. It shows the date and the time of day in one corner of the picture. Without this feature, video pictures would be useless as evidence.

Eye in the Sky

Sometimes crowds don't stay in one spot – they move. A protest march or demonstration is a good example of this. When people are on the move, fixed cameras are not much use. In this situation, the police sometimes use a camera operated from a

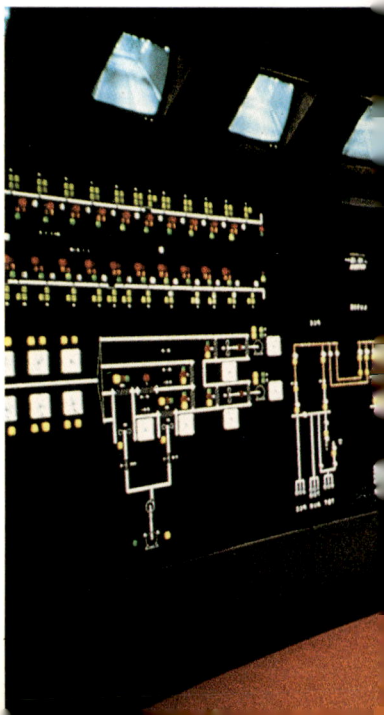

helicopter. The camera acts as any "eye in the sky." This eye keeps a lookout for medical emergencies and other possible trouble.

A Highway Monitor

In some European countries, including Great Britain, highways are sometimes monitored by police cameras. A video system linked to a computer is attached to a bridge over a highway and aimed so that it can see every license plate as cars pass underneath. With the help of the computer, the system can not only see the plates, but also "read" them. The computer is able to check every license number to determine whether it belongs to a car listed as lost or stolen. The police may not recover stolen vehicles instantly, but this is often able to put them on the right track.

Below: CCTV screens allow a single controller to survey a vast amount of traffic.

Doing It Yourself

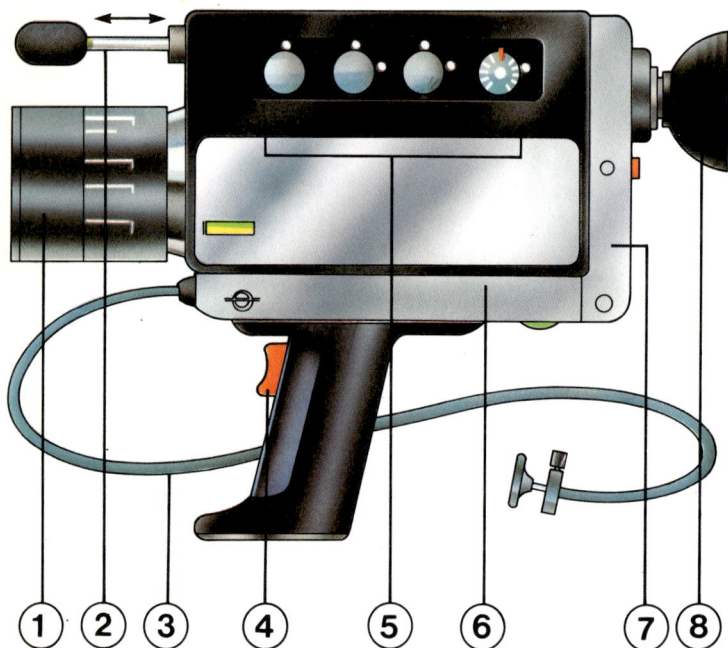

① ② ③ ④ ⑤ ⑥ ⑦⑧

THE SUPER-8 CAMERA

1 Zoom lens
2 Microphone
3 Cable release for stop-
   frame work
4 Grip and trigger
5 Control panel
6 Battery compartment
7 Cassette compartment
8 Adjustable eyepiece

Making your own films and
videos is an expensive hobby.
The best way for young
enthusiasts to start is to join
a school or youth film or
video club.

Super-8
In 1965 Kodak introduced a
new amateur moviemaking
system. It was based on 8-mm
film housed inside a cassette.
Super-8, as it is called,
proved to be much simpler to

use than previous systems. In 1972 a **sound stripe** was added. Super-8 is now a well-tried, reasonably cheap, moviemaking system.

You can film almost anything with modern Super-8 equipment. The basic difference between 8-mm film and the 35-mm professional film has to do with projection. You cannot project 8-mm film across a large public hall with any success. But for showing at home, or in a classroom, it's fine.

Getting Started

A suitable subject and reasonably bright light are all you need to start filming with a Super-8 camera. You can find operating instructions in a number of books and magazines. They offer detailed guidance on Super-8 moviemaking. Schools, community centers, and youth organizations sometimes set up Super-8 clubs.

When the film has been processed, you will need a Super-8 projector. This *threads* the film automatically.

Below: This animation was produced very quickly and simply by children, drawing directly onto clear 35-mm film with spirit-based pens.

If things go well, you can get more ambitious. Then other items, such as a **cutter** and a **splicer**, may be on your shopping list.

Film Clubs

Production is not the only side of moviemaking that can be handled by amateurs. Screening can also be done on an amateur basis. The film size most suitable for amateur projectionists is 16-

Below: Film clubs can choose any of thousands of 16-mm films from many different countries. Just reading the catalogs can be fun.

mm. By using 16-mm film, you can project a fairly large image. It will be seen clearly by 100 or more people.

Many schools, youth organizations and community centers own a 16-mm projector. It is not as easy to operate as an 8-mm projector. This is because each reel has to be threaded by hand. But there's usually someone in charge of the machine who can do this, and show you how.

There are film clubs in towns all over the country. The seating and print quality are usually not as good as those in a movie theater. But members have the luxury of

SCHOOL FILM SOCIETY

This month's films:
ORPHÉE — 7.30
PSYCHO — 8.30
ALEXANDER NEVSKY — 7.3
INTOLERANCE —
LES ENFANTS DU PARADIS — 5.00 FRIDAY

16mm FILM Catalogue ★

Films for Hire

choosing the movies they want to see, when they want to see them.

Available Films

There are over 8,000 feature-length movies for film clubs to choose from. They range from silent comedies made in the 1920s to space fantasies of the 1980s. In additon to American movies, there are movies made in many other countries all around the world.

There are also thousands of short films, or "shorts." These offer an even greater variety of style and subject than the features do. This is because a lot of them have been made independently,

Above: *Jobs for the Girls*, made by a British film co-op, is an independent film about a young woman who wants to be a motorcycle mechanic.

rather than by the big studios. A short subject made in this way can be original and adventurous. Some even poke fun at the big studio "blockbusters." A short called *Hardware Wars*, for example, satirizes the *Star Wars* movies.

Other short subjects listed in the catalogs include **animation**, travelogues, documentaries, experimental films, and films from the 1890s by Méliès and the Lumière brothers.

The Camcorder

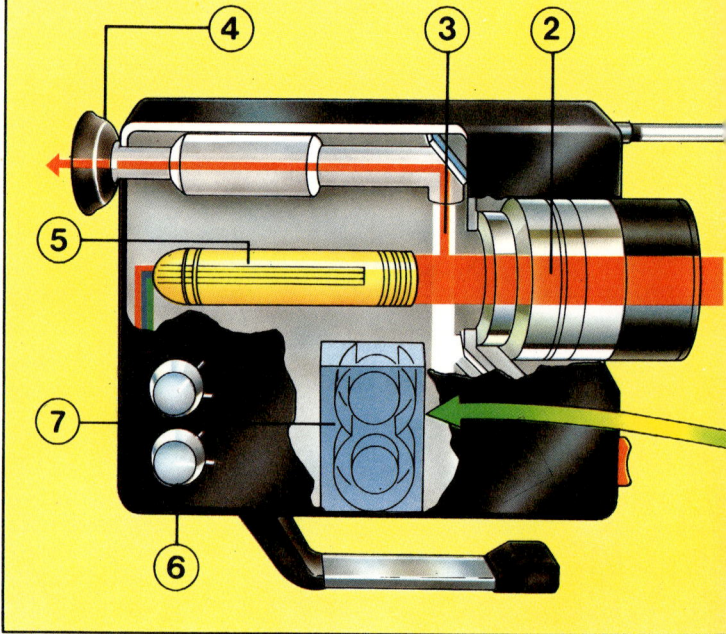

Even after the invention of the $\frac{3}{4}$-inch (2-cm) U-Matic cassette system, video cameras were much too expensive for most people. There were also too many things that could go wrong with them, and they were heavy.

A number of lighter and simpler systems have been developed. The most recent of these is the **camcorder**. As its name suggests, this combines a video camera with a recorder. A typical camcorder weighs about five pounds (two kg) and produces cassettes that can be played back on an ordinary home VCR. It can be plugged into the electricity supply or run on batteries.

With a camcorder, home movies are easier to make than ever before. Film was usually used for special occasions. But the camcorder's relatively low cost and simplicity mean that everyday family activities can now be recorded on video. Playback is easy, too. You don't need to

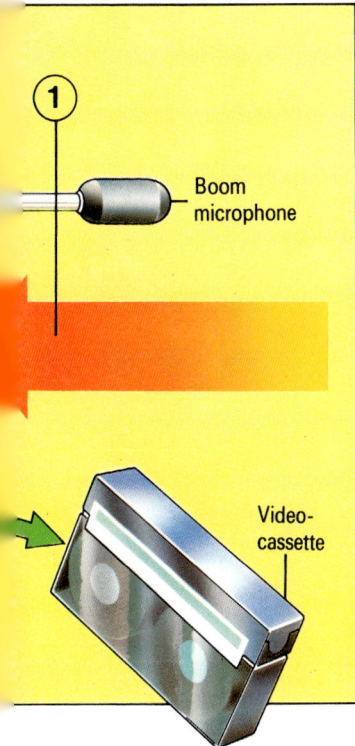

Boom microphone

Video-cassette

Light (1) from the subject being recorded passes through the lens (2), to the "beamsplitter" (3). From here, a section of the beam of light is sent to the eyepiece (4). By this means, the user sees exactly what the lens is seeing, even though the eyepiece is higher up. The rest of the light beam goes through a "saticon tube" (5), which breaks it up into its three colors – red, blue and green. After adjustment by the controls (6), the image is recorded on a mini-cassette (7). Sound from all directions is recorded by the microphone, which is on a boom so that it can get close to the main subject.

have a projector and screen to show your "home movies." All that is required is a VCR and an ordinary TV screen.

Camcorder or Super-8?

The camcorder has some obvious advantages over Super-8. It can record continuously for at least an hour. No time or money has to be spent in processing. And it uses the TV screen that's already in the home.

Camcorder's one big dis-advantage is in editing. Super-8 film editing can be done quite successfully at home with the right equipment. But smooth video editing is only possible with a costly professional suite. At home, a rough editing job can be done by borrowing someone else's VCR and linking it to your own. You can then transfer selected shots from one to the other. This is known as "crash-editing," and the results are messy to watch.

For the dramatic effects that can be achieved by editing, Super-8 still has the advantage over a camcorder.

Above: Video can easily be taken on location; for example, to get opinions and comments from a person on the street.

Video Workshops

In many places people have come together to work on independent video productions. These groups often run courses for young people.

The aim of such a course is not to produce masterpieces. It is to provide firsthand experience with video.

Typically, a course will start with instruction on how to operate video equipment. Then the group will discuss ideas for filming. Finally, a plan for a video is put together, and the young people start shooting.

Youth clubs and schools can use video in many different ways. One practical use is in preparing for job interviews. A mock interview is recorded. This not only gives young people a chance to operate cameras. It also allows them, on playback, to see themselves as a prospective employer would.

Video Scratching

"Video scratching" can be fun. It involves mixing together an assortment of TV pictures with a new soundtrack. The simplest way of going about this is to connect an audio cassette player to a VCR. Play a music tape, and set the VCR to record. Then switch from one TV channel to another in time with the music. You might get snatches of a soap opera, a wildlife documentary, a cartoon, or a political interview. The music replaces the original soundtrack. It helps to bind the assorted clips together.

Another, more complicated technique uses two connected VCRs. On one tape is a collection of choice clips. They may have been recorded over a long period of time. Selected clips are then transferred to another videotape to suit the music or the words of the song. In between the pictures a fuzzy screen will appear. But then scratch video isn't meant to look like smoothly edited film.

Animation and Special Effects

King Kong, Mickey Mouse, Bugs Bunny, the Pink Panther – some of the most famous movie stars have been drawings and models. These and others have brought pleasure to millions. But creating them gets more expensive every day. Now computers have begun to replace human hands.

24 Pink Panthers a Second
Making a cartoon, or animation, is based on the fact that all movies are made up of still pictures.

In traditional animation, photographs are taken of a series of drawings. Each drawing is very slightly different from the one before it. When they are projected, the characters or objects appear to move. They become "animated." The drawings are

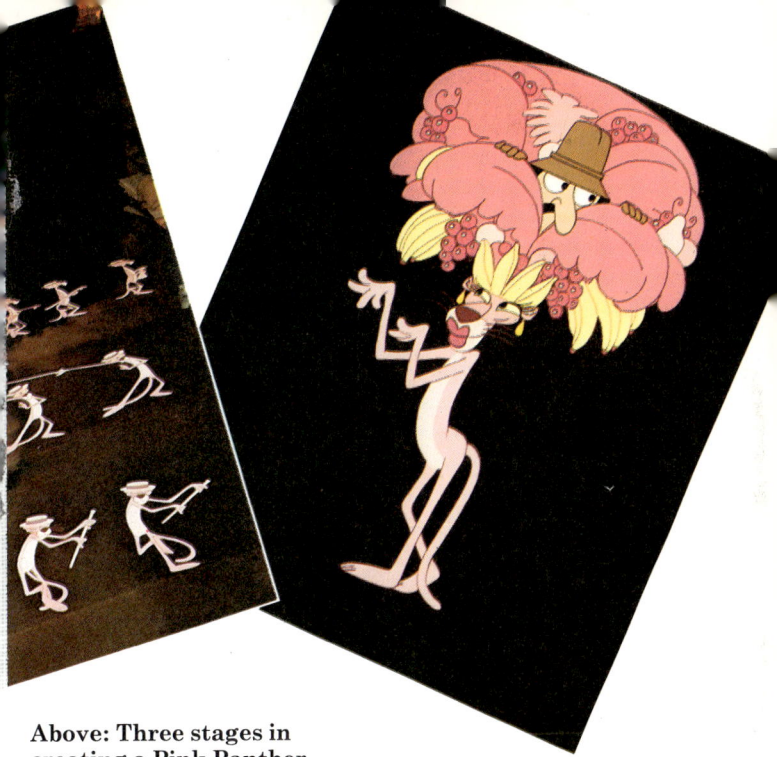

Above: Three stages in creating a Pink Panther cartoon. The original sketch is drawn onto "cels," then photographed onto film.

done on separate sheets of transparent film, called **cels**. The film is projected at 24 frames per second. So 24 drawings are needed in order to create one second of screen time.

The Magic of Disney

The most famous creator of animated films was Walt Disney. His animators put a tremendous amount of detail into their drawings. Leaves rustled in the breeze, transparent drops of water splashed in ponds, and reflections and shadows were used to create dramatic effects. It took Disney four years to produce *Snow White and the Seven Dwarfs* using this approach.

Thirty years later, this style of full animation is too expensive – even for the Disney studios. Cartoons produced for television have resorted to partial animation.

Model SFX

In fantasy films it is impossible to stage everything in front of the cameras "for real." This is where **special effects** (SFX) come in. Animation is considered to be a special effect when it is seen in the same frame as live action.

Instead of a series of drawings, models are usually used for this kind of special effect. Model animation works in much the same way as drawn animation. **Stop-frame** photography takes a series of still pictures. As in cartoons, the action in each frame is slightly advanced on the one preceding it. But the animator does not have to make a new model for each frame. Instead, the model is made flexible enough to be used again and again. Only the position of the limbs or body is altered from shot to shot.

A Sympathetic Monster

The most famous example of model animation is over 50 years old. King Kong, the

Left: Kong was billed as "The Eighth Wonder of the World." At the time, amazed audiences didn't know how he had been brought to life.

giant ape who struck terror and pity into the hearts of millions, was in reality a little aluminum skeleton. It was covered with rubber, cotton, latex and rabbit fur.

His creator was a man named Willis O'Brien. O'Brien's greatest success was in making Kong into a real character in the film, not just a roaring monster. He gave the ape mannerisms, facial expressions, and moving eyes.

Appearing in the same settings as the actors, Kong seemed about 60 feet (18 m) tall. A variety of methods created this effect. In some shots, the size of everything else in the frame – huts, trees, the Empire State Building – was scaled down. Even the human heroine was replaced by a four-inch (10-cm) model at times. For other shots, a full-size model of Kong's head and shoulders, and one paw, was built. The result was very convincing, and the movie became a classic.

Skeletons and Snakes

O'Brien's methods were developed over the years by one of his assistants – Ray Harryhausen. In *Jason and the Argonauts*, for example, Harryhausen animated a famous sequence in which Jason fights seven skeleton warriors. This was a very complicated job, because each skeleton had four limbs and a head. That meant that for each frame, 35 different parts had to be moved.

Most producers now consider this kind of special effect to be too expensive. They are turning to electronics as a cheaper alternative.

Above: For certain scenes, a full-scale model of Kong's head and shoulders was built. There was also a wire-operated paw.

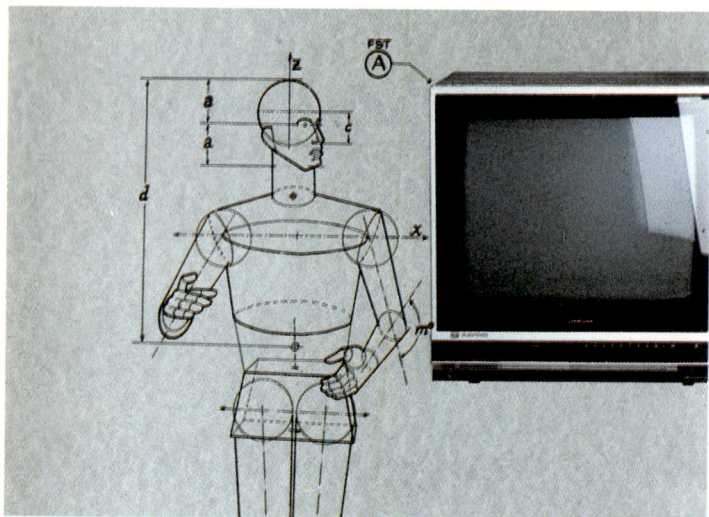

Video Animation

Until very recently, smooth, frame-by-frame animation was impossible with video. Now, a **single-frame** ½-inch (1.3 cm) video system is available. It has by no means replaced film in animation. It has, however, become a useful assistant.

Video animation is an excellent learning aid. Students can quickly rough out a series of drawings and tape them, frame by frame. By playing them back, it is possible to see whether they "come to life" properly.

This process of trying out drawings by putting them onto video is known as a **line test**. Experienced animators find line tests just as useful as students. Before single-frame video was available, they used to have to test their work by flipping through their drawings as they would a flip book.

Add a Computer
Computers have made all kinds of things possible for the animator.

Computers can think only in terms of numbers. So the drawing has to be **digitized** (changed into numbers) before the computer can do anything with it. There are two ways of doing this. Instructions can be sent to the computer screen using a keyboard. Or, an outline can be drawn with a special pen onto an electronic pad.

Instructions can then be sent to make changes to the drawing on the screen. These include "squash," "stretch," "wobble," "bend," "twist," "spiral," and "explode."

A computer has a built-in memory. This gives it another great advantage over the camera and recorder. Line testing can be done in a much more sophisticated way. Once a sequence is stored in the computer's memory, it can be replayed at any speed. Individual frames can be added, taken out, duplicated, or changed around. Professional animators may feel limited by the lifelessness of the computer's other routines. But they find this type of help extremely useful.

Below: Max Headroom, smooth-talking presenter of his own TV rock video show, is entirely the product of computer animation.

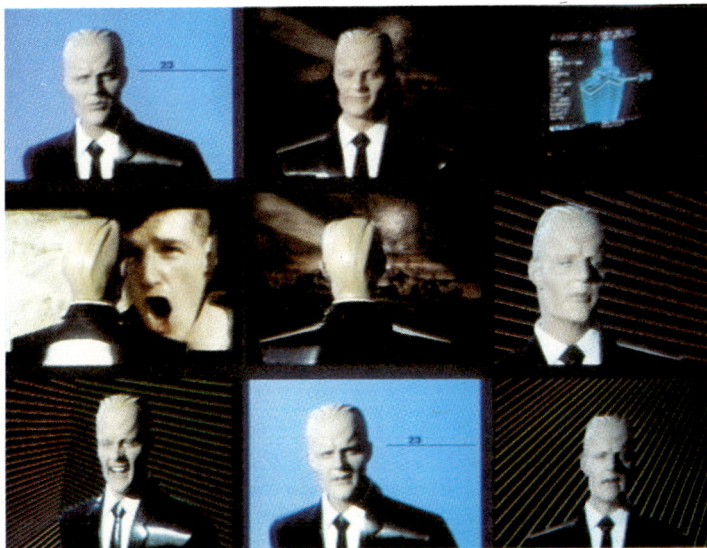

77

Computers and the Movies

New technology in the 1980s helped to produce *Tron* and *The Last Starfighter*. These were two feature-length movies that used a lot of computer animation. Most of the effects could have been produced by tradtional methods of animation. But these methods would have taken twenty times longer.

Computer Starfighters

Frames of film that have been produced by computer can vary a great deal in quality. This depends on the number of **polygons** in them. A polygon is the smallest possible detail from which the picture is made up. Even in the two years between *Tron* and *The Last Starfighter* there was a big change in computer powers. In *Tron* there were never more than 30,000 polygons in any one frame. *The Last Starfighter*, however, used a CRAY X-MP, the most powerful computer in the world at that time. The animators were able to compose frames that contained an average of one million polygons. This resul-

ted in a much smoother picture.

Because of this difference, the images in *Tron* look "computerized." They are meant to, because the action takes place inside the mind of a computer. In *The Last Starfighter*, however, they are meant to look like real objects.

Right: One of the computerized sequences from *Tron*.

78

In-betweening

Another advance took place between the making of these two films. This was in the time it took to produce each frame of animated film.

After the drawings had been digitized, programmers gave the computer the **key frames**. These show the position of all the objects at the main points of the action. The computer was then told to "in-between." This meant drawing in all the frames needed to take the action from one key frame to the next stage of the action.

For the animated sequence in *Tron*, the computer took an average of five minutes to produce each in-between frame. For *The Last Starfighter*, this job was reduced to an average of two minutes. Even so, it meant that each second of screen time took at least 48 minutes to create.

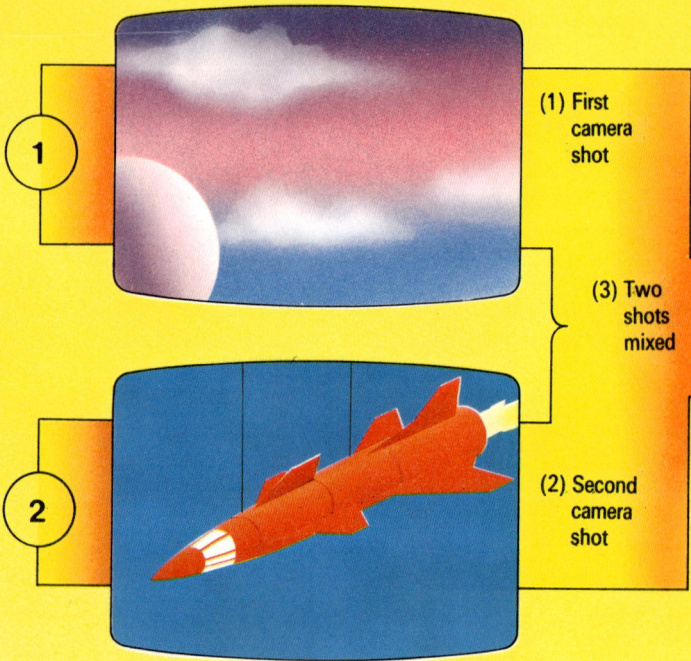

(1) First camera shot

(3) Two shots mixed

(2) Second camera shot

Video Effects

Television studios now have a vast range of electronic effects available to them. Unlike film effects, many of these are meant to be obvious to the audience. When a TV announcer is suddenly picked up, enclosed in a small box, and sent whirling around, or when one scene changes to another by being turned over like a page in a book – such effects are part of the entertainment.

A completely different kind of video effect is *not* meant to be noticed by the viewer. This is achieved by a device known as **chromakey**. Chromakey can be used to combine a person or object from one place, and a setting

Just as chromakey can remove all traces of a given color from a frame, this "painting by numbers" effect is achieved by replacing different levels of brightness in a picture with a different color.

3

Double shot effect using chromakey

from another, into a single image.

The person or object to be "transported" is normally in front of a blue background. Blue is chosen because it is almost entirely absent from human skin coloring. The chromakey then removes all blue from the frame. All that remains in the frame is the person or object. The missing background is then replaced by an appropriate scene.

Chromakey has all sorts of dramatic uses. For example, it can make someone appear to be very small. There is no need to build oversized props. This is done by filming the person from a long distance with one camera. Another camera shows the setting, for example a forest, in closeup. When the two pictures are merged, the person may appear to be no bigger than a flower.

Animatronics

When Rick Baker was given the first Makeup Oscar in 1982, he had in fact branched out beyond makeup. He was using a technique now known as **animatronics**.

For a long time, Baker and John Landis, the director, had wanted to make a movie in which a man would change into a werewolf before the audience's very eyes, during a continuous take. Up until then, such transformations had been done by dissolves. These faded one stage of the transformation into the next, and so on.

When Baker and Landis first had the idea, no technique existed to make it possible. Nothing like it had ever been done before.

The idea became a real possibility when an invention called "Smooth-on" became available. Like foam rubber but far more elastic, Smooth-on looks just like human flesh. In *An American Werewolf in London*, it was

used to show the actor's hand growing into a wolf claw.

The actor's real hand was kept out of camera range. The hand that changed was a construction full of cables and plastic tubing. It was covered with Smooth-on. The cables were a little like the brake cables on a bike. They went up inside the fingers so

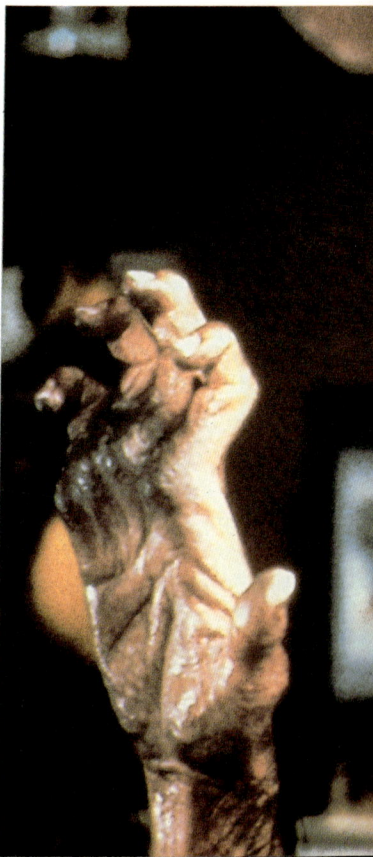

Right: Animatronics in action in *An American Werewolf in London*. The actor's real hand is below the frame, out of sight.

that operators could make them move. The tubing provided the "growth."

Inside each end of the tubing was a syringe. The one at the operator's end was much larger than the one inside the palm. When the operator forced the large plunger down, air pressure traveled through the tubing and pushed the smaller plunger outward. The elasticity of the Smooth-on absorbed this force without breaking, and the hand was able to "grow" into a claw.

This technique and other similar ones have been used frequently in recent movies. *Greystoke*, *Starman* and *The Company of Wolves* have all used some form of animatronics.

As it happens, the Oscar definition of "Makeup" has now been changed. It excludes animatronic effects.

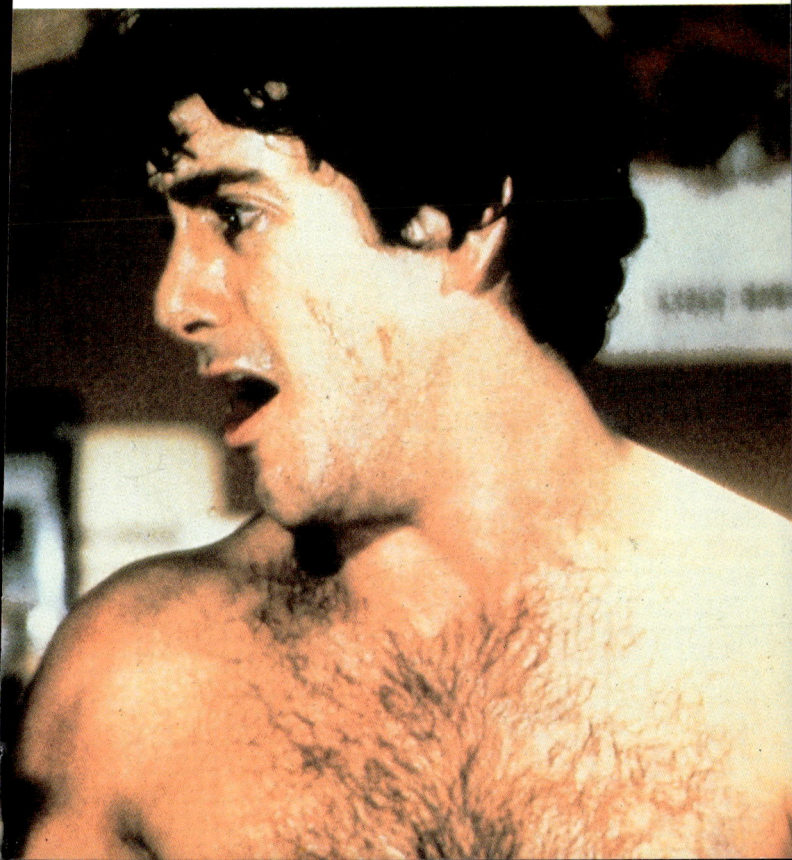

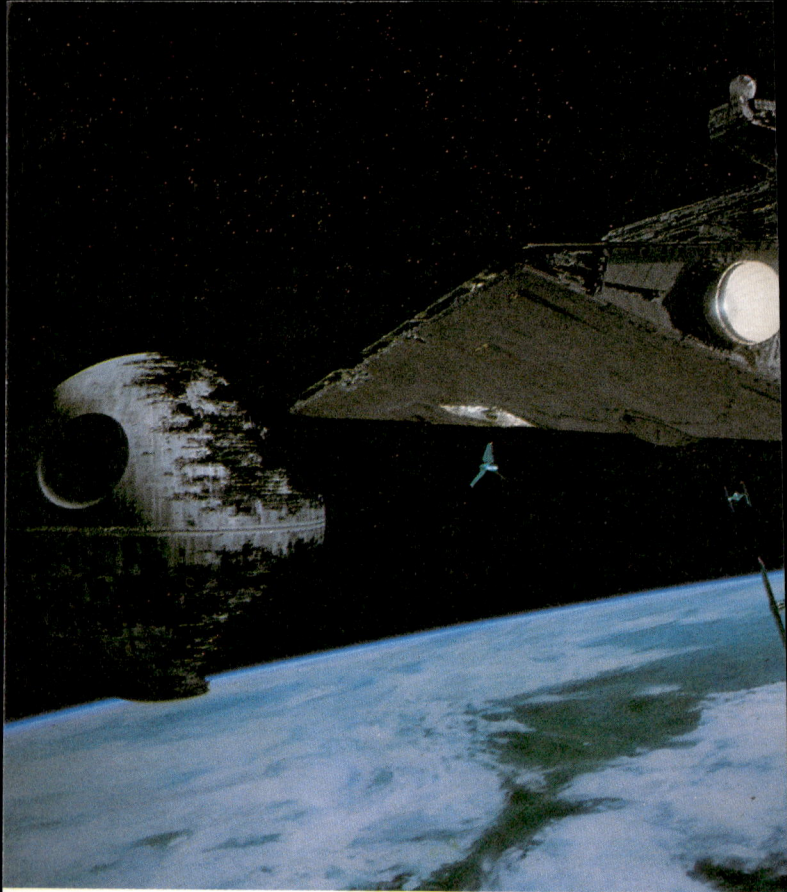

Light and Magic

Many recent blockbusters owe a great deal of their success to a California company called Industrial Light and Magic (ILM). It is a movie studio – but actors never work there. Its job is to bring to life creatures and effects that are barely im- aginable. ILM will use any technology to do this, old or new. It is the special effects capital of the world.

ILM specializes in making its effects look completely realistic. For this purpose, it has developed some new approaches. One of these is

Left: Some shots from *Return of the Jedi* used 63 different model spaceships. The final print composited 170 separate pieces of film. It took weeks to do, but lasts only two seconds on the screen.

second, will be just a little bit blurred around the edges. This actually makes it seem more realistic. The speeding bike sequence in *Return of the Jedi* was created mainly in this way.

Another specialty of ILM involves **compositing**. This means bringing together all sorts of images from various sources. The mine train chase in *Indiana Jones and the Temple of Doom* is a good example. It consists of model work created at ILM, live action footage shot thousands of miles away in London, and line animation of flying sparks. At ILM these three sources were edited together in a single image.

Even more complicated was the compositing used in the space battle sequences of the *Star Wars* films. All the spacecraft seen in the finished version had to be controlled and photographed individually. One scene, in *Return of the Jedi*, is the most complicated special effects shot ever achieved.

called "Go-motion." It works in much the same way as stop-frame. But each frame of film is exposed for one full second, rather than for 1/48th of a second as is normal. The idea is that if the film is exposed for a whole second, the object being photographed will shake slightly. The result, when projected at the normal 24 frames per

Things to Come

Film and video, as we have seen, are sometimes rivals and sometimes partners. Now that video projection systems and large, high-quality TV screens are being developed, video seems all set to invade the movie theaters. Meanwhile, both film and video, linked with computers, are exploring new avenues of education and entertainment.

In the late 1970s, projecting videotape onto a theater-sized screen became possible.

The basic idea involved three separate "guns." Each projects one of the primary light colors – red, blue, and green. When they hit the screen, these colors combine to re-create the video picture.

The quality of these enlarged TV pictures varies from system to system, and from tape to tape. Some people find them too fuzzy and faint under any circumstances. Other people argue that the best quality videotapes produce an image as good as, but

not better than, 16-mm film. A few "video movie theaters" have come into operation. For theater managers, video offers a big advantage over film. It does away with the expense of hiring a projectionist, since anyone can slot a cassette into a VCR.

The World's Largest Television

At the Tokyo Science Expo '85, the Sony Corporation displayed the Sony Jumbotron, the largest TV screen in the world. It contained new advances in screen size and in picture quality. The screen is 130 feet (40 m) wide, and 80 feet (25 m) high. That makes its total surface area more than three times as great as that of an IMAX screen. According to Sony, the Jumbotron can produce a clearer image than any home TV set.

It seems unlikely that Jumbotron screens will be installed very widely, except in sports stadiums and at racetracks. For theatrical entertainment they are simply too big and expensive.

Left: In some discos and nightclubs, sport and rock videos are now projected as background entertainment.

Below: A Rank Hi-Beam video projector, showing the three separate colorguns.

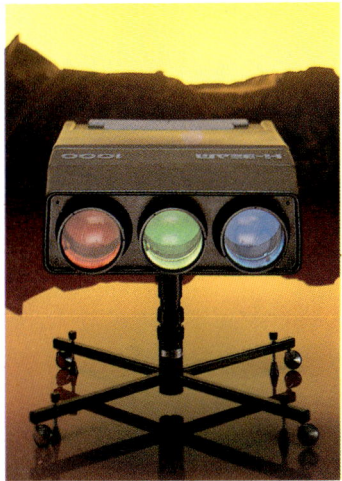

But it does show that high-quality video pictures on the big screen are not far off. It remains to be seen whether the experience they will offer an audience can compare with 70-mm film or IMAX.

Future animation

In the field of computer animation, programmers hope to become as good at animating pictures of living things as they are at machinery. For this, they will need a computer with a certain level of artificial intelligence.

Above: In *Star Wars*, Princess Leia sends a hologram of herself to Obi Wan Kenobi in a plea for help.

Discs and Lasers

Videocassettes are once again available in plastic disc form, this time for the home. A videodisc contains digitized picture and sound information on its spiral track. The disc is spun at 1,800 revolutions per minute. A diamond or sapphire **stylus** "reads" the information and turns it into pictures and sound.

Compared with tape, a videodisc has various advantages. The picture and sound quality are higher. It is cheaper, and lasts longer. And it is possible to move quickly from one part of the recording to another. It cannot be used for home recording, however, and it requires its own special screen.

Another playback-only system is called LaserVision. It has a plastic disc coated with a shiny metallized layer. The picture-information is read, not by a stylus, but by a very narrow laser beam.

Linked to a computer, LaserVision is ideal for educational purposes. The computer knows what is on each of the 108,000 frames on a one-hour disc, and any frame or sequence can be found within seconds. It can be held for as long as it is wanted.

Holograms and 3-D TV
When used with film, lasers can also produce three-dimensional images known as **holograms**. Holograms are created by splitting a laser beam down the middle. One half of the beam is directed at the film. The other half of the beam strikes the object, then is reflected off onto the film. When the film is illuminated by laser light, the image is recreated with depth as well as width and height. The future development of holography, linked with computer control, may make 3-D movies and TV possible.

Some experts predict that the next century will see film and video replaced by computers and digitized recording. Whatever the form, moving pictures are sure to endure as entertainment, art, and as a visual record of our time.

Below: In the near future, 3-D TV, which does not require the viewer to wear special glasses, may be successfully developed.

Glossary

Animation Making drawings and models appear to have life.

Animatronics The art of making things seem to live, or grow, by means of electronics and modern chemical substances.

Audio Having to do with sound and hearing.

Credits Information about who has done what in the making of a particular film.

Cutter A device for cutting a piece of film cleanly, at the required point.

Deep focus lens A particular type of lens which can see things clearly, both in the background and in the foreground at the same time.

Digitized Described in terms of numbers, so that a computer can understand.

Dissolve When one film image fades into a different one, so that for a short time both images can be seen on the screen together.

Documentary A type of film that shows events that occur naturally; events that have not been staged specially for the camera's benefit.

Editing The process of cutting out or rearranging various parts of the material that has been recorded.

Electron The smallest component of matter.

Electron beam tube A glass tube inside which a stream of electrons moves in a vacuum.

Exposure The time needed for the image to be satisfactorily recorded.

Film stock The actual rolls of plastic that make up film.

Focus A control on a camera which, by moving the lens, enables the operator to see the main subject clearly, without any blurred edges.

Footage A certain length of exposed film.

Frame One complete picture on a piece of film or video.

Freeze-frame A control mechanism on a VCR, which allows the operator to look closely at one particular frame.

High-definition Extremely clear and bright, with no fuzzy edges.

Lace To thread a film correctly through a projector, from one spool to another, so that it is ready to be projected.

Lens A circle of glass or plastic, thicker in the middle than at the edges. It bends beams of light and so controls the way a camera "sees."

Limelight A brilliant white light produced by heating a piece of lime.

Post-production The work that is done on a piece of film or video after the actual recording or taping is finished.

Print Film stock that has been exposed and processed.

Projection When an image is thrown onto a screen as a result of a beam of light passing through a piece of film or glass slide.

Recording head That part of a VCR at which the picture information is actually transferred to or from the tape.

Remote control Command over a machine's operation by means of signals sent from a distance.

Shutter A device that keeps light out of a camera. For a photograph to be taken, the shutter has to be quickly removed and replaced.

Single-frame The same as stop-frame.

Sound stripe A magnetized strip running along the edge of a roll of film. Sound can be recorded onto it, and it then becomes the soundtrack.

Splicer A device that makes it possible to stick pieces of film together smoothly and accurately.

Spool A circular framework, made of plastic or metal, which keeps the film tightly rolled.

Stop-frame A technique widely used in animation. It consists of exposing only one frame at a time, and altering the drawing or model between each frame.

Storyboard A plan that shows, by means of drawings, the key scenes of the material to be shot.

Stylus A tiny piece of diamond or sapphire which follows the groove on a disk.

Supply spool The spool which the tape is on at the start of recording or playback.

Synchronized Organized so that two or more things happen at the same time; for instance in film, when the sound of speech is made to match lip movements.

Take The filming of a particular shot.

Takeup spool The spool on which the tape is collected after it has passed through the VCR.

Telecine transfer A professional process by which images and sound can be moved from film to video, or from video to film.

Tracking shot A shot during which the camera is moved along during filming.

Zoom-in When the space between lenses in a camera is changed so that part of the image seems to come closer.

Index

Page numbers in *italics* refer to illustrations